BRAVE IS NOW

BRAVE  NOW

THE ART OF BEING BRAVE

JENNIFER ZAROU

gatekeeper press

Columbus, Ohio

Brave Is Now: The Art of Being Brave

Published by Gatekeeper Press
2167 Stringtown Rd, Suite 109
Columbus, OH 43123-2989
www.GatekeeperPress.com

ISBN (hardcover): 9781642378689

To Julia & Jenna
You are the bravest girls I know.
I love you,
Mom

Preface

WELCOME TO A LITTLE PIECE of my Brave Is Now journey. About six years ago I was on the verge of making some very important life changes, some by choice, and some as a result of my recent cancer diagnosis. I was riddled with uncertainty, self-doubt and fear at the prospect of having to navigate the uncertainty that lie ahead, knowing, as a single parent my decisions would also impact my two young daughters. I had clarity in my head about what I needed to do, but my body was paralyzed—cemented down in the terror of the unknown. During a scheduled visit with my doctor, I found out that my cancer had become more aggressive. At that moment, I realized it was time to be brave. I knew I didn't have time for discussions, emotions, fear and uncertainty—in that moment I needed to be brave. Brave Is Now is what came to my mind, and to my mouth and has been the motivation that has kept me moving forward.

We all have our own Brave Is Now story, the need and urgency to inhale the uncertainty and exhale the brave in our everyday lives. Now more than ever, the call to be brave is paramount. I am sharing my Brave Is Now story with you with the hopes that you will realize your own and share it with me at www.braveisnow.com

Brave Is Now!

Jennifer Zarou

Rock
bottom
can either be
about how far
you've fallen
or about how
high
you will rise up
the choice is
yours~

BRAVE IS NOW

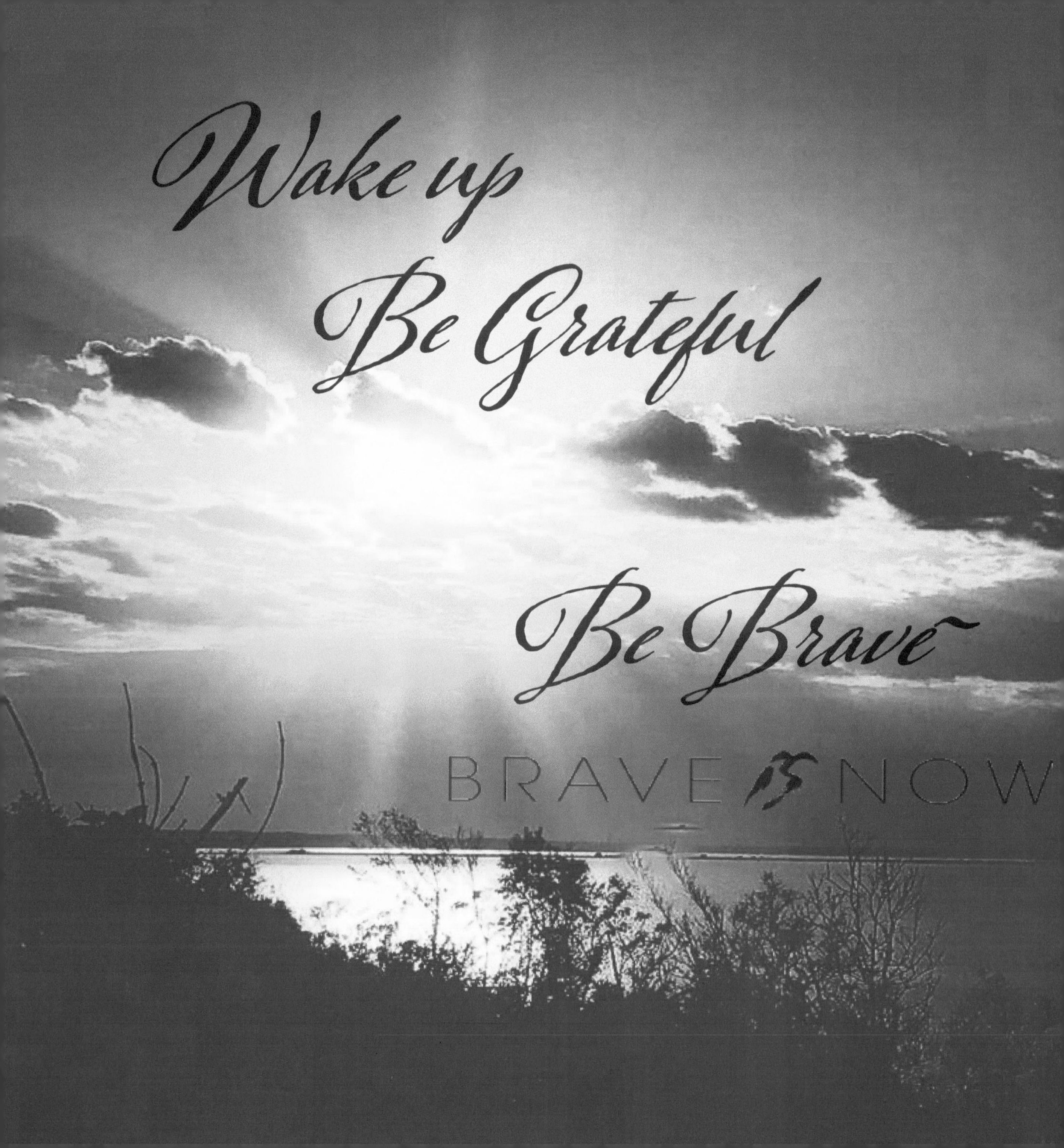
Wake up
Be Grateful
Be Brave
BRAVE NOW

Be
Inspired
everyday~

BRAVE NOW

Be your own
kind of beautiful~

BRAVE ♭ NOW

Being breathless
is not so much about having
less breath
but more about having
too much awe!

Be brave enough
to lose your breath~

BRAVE *IS* NOW

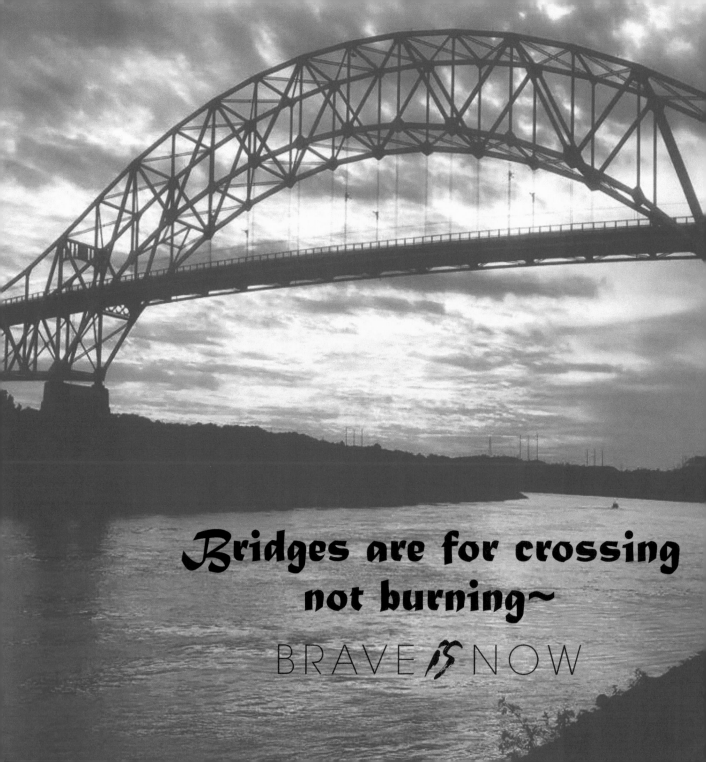

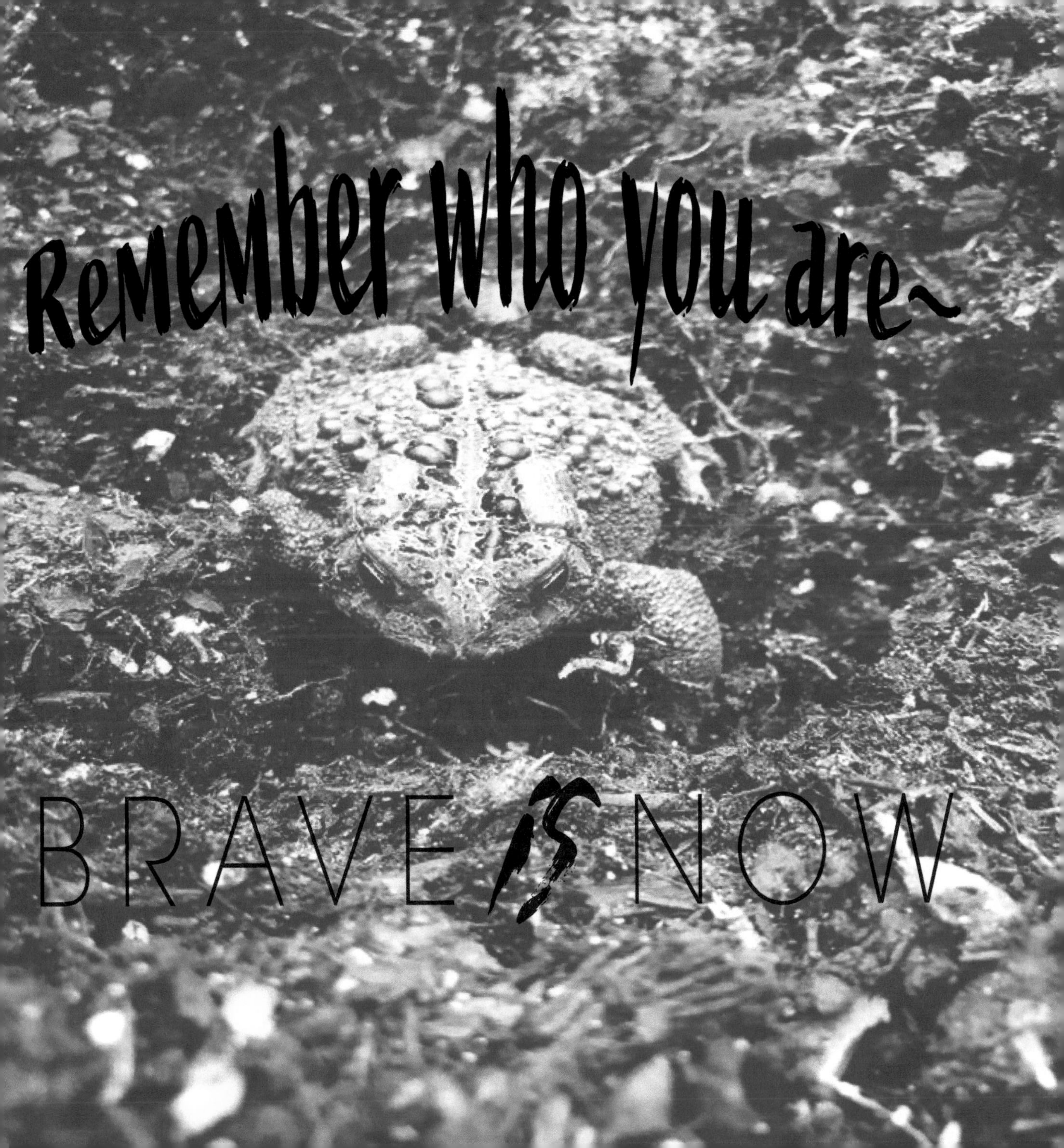
Remember who you are~
BRAVE is NOW

Celebrate Everything~

BRAVE IS NOW

Love makes us eternal~

BRAVE IS NOW

Never give up
on
gratitude~

BRAVE is NOW

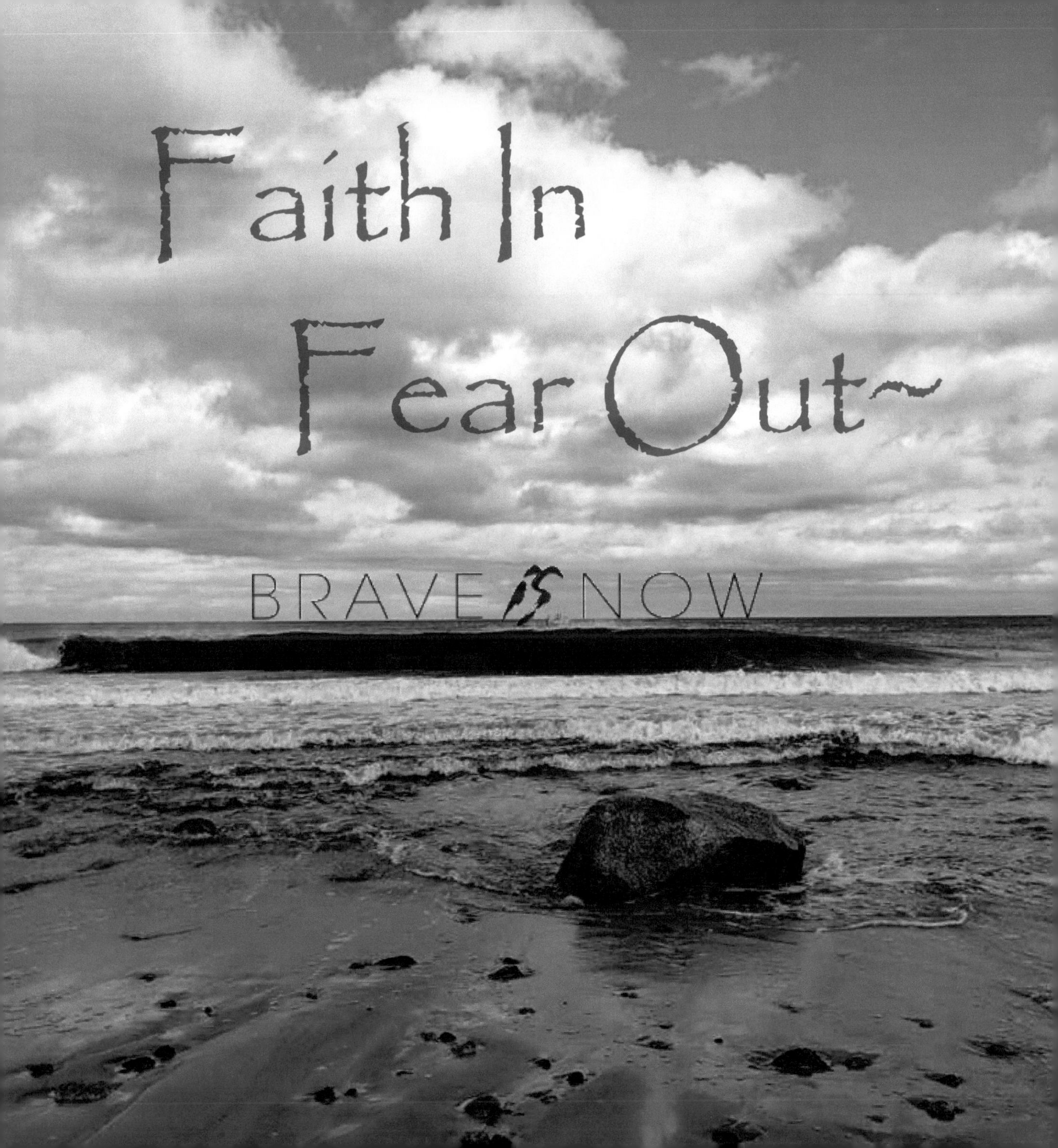
Faith In
Fear Out~
BRAVE IS NOW

Make
wherever
you are
your own
happy
place~

BRAVE IS NOW

No matter how far you go
always remember
how far you've come~

BRAVE IS NOW

Let
love
in~

BRAVE IS NOW

If It keeps
you awake at
night
it's either time
to move forard or
time
to move on~

BRAVE IS NOW

There is absolutely no reason ~
you can't have it all

There
is no
limit
to how
big
your dreams can be~

BRAVE *IS* NOW

Pride is infinite~

BRAVE IS NOW

It's
always
the right
time
to do the
right
thing~

BRAVE IS NOW

Don't be afraid to let your soul shine through

BRAVE IS NOW

Silence
may not
be the answer
you want
but it is
an
answer~

BRAVE NOW

At the end of the day
we are only as brave
as the stories we live~

BRAVE IS NOW

Success is being able to say
you would
do it all again
the exact same way
because you love
who you've become~

Freedom comes when you are brave enough to untie the ties that bind you~

The pain from
staying
will last long after
the pain from
leaving
when it's time to go
your heart will know ~

BRAVE IS NOW

The
heart
remembers
what
time
foregts~

BRAVE *is* NOW

Your truth will always find you~

You will
always
get
what
you need
when
you are brave
enough
to believe ~

BRAVE *IS* NOW

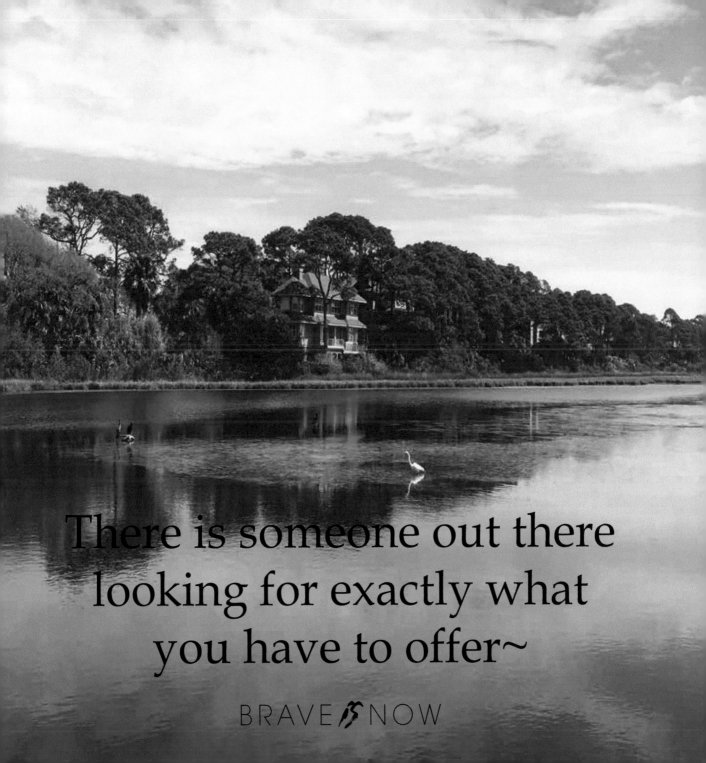

There is someone out there
looking for exactly what
you have to offer~

BRAVE NOW

It's who you choose
to share the view with
that matters ~

Let the beauty inside be bigger than what they see on the outside~

Things are not always what they seem
Sometimes they are better~

BRAVE is NOW

When you believe in your direction you will do anything to get there~

BRAVE IS NOW

BE YOUR
OWN
BEST
COMPANION~

BRAVE IS NOW

Some days you might feel
like you will cry
for a hundred years
for a thousand different reasons
in a million different ways
but I promise
when the crying stops
you will still be
the one beautiful
unbroken being
you have always been~

Don't believe everything you think~

BRAVE IS NOW

When it's apples and oranges
be the dragonfruit~

BRAVE IS NOW

If you
have to go back
a second time
to fix what didn't work the first time
make sure it's your last-
time~

Only a real hero can teach you how to be your own~

BRAVE NOW

You can always
change
the way you think
about something
but **NEVER**
abandon
how it makes you feel~

BRAVE is NOW

Act
as
if
until
it
is~

BRAVE IS NOW

Sometimes the best way to see in is to look out~

BRAVE*NOW

You are not broken
You are in repair~

BRAVE IS NOW

Author Bio

Jennifer Zarou is a psychotherapist, single mother and dog rescuer. She survived cancer twice and is currently undergoing chemotherapy for Leukemia. As the mother of two young adult girls, and having just been diagnosed with her third cancer, Jennifer became obsessed with teaching her girls how to be brave with life, knowing that if her treatment didn't work, they would have to be. The thought of not being able to watch her girls grow and navigate through their own lives consumed Jennifer's thoughts, and she began a "Brave" journal that she hoped would one day act as her voice if hers was no longer.

The Brave Journal soon turned into *Brave Is Now*, a combination of photographs and brave inspirations, that reinforce the importance and immediacy of being brave. Jennifer never realized that what had begun as a lesson in bravery for her girls, would also become the anchor of bravery she needed to not only survive but to thrive. This book is *Brave Is Now*.